"God Hears My Song"
First edition 2021
Copyright © With Love From Above Books, Inc 2021
All rights reserved.

Edited by Glenys Nellist, Sheri Wall, Andrea Ketchelmeier, and developmental editor Karen Austin.

Library of Congress Control Number: 2021949437

ISBN paperback 978-1-7379652-0-6
ISBN hardback 978-1-7379652-1-3
ISBN audiobook 978-1-7379652-2-0

Dedicated to all children:

GOD
HEARS MY SONG

Written by
Heather Lean

Illustrated by
Yorris Handoko

Dear God, I know you hear my song.
I feel your love—it keeps me strong.

You calm my troubles, fears, and fright
To help me know I'm safe at night.

I'm glad you shared the world with me,
And all things blooming wild and free.

The grass that tickles toes and feet,
The springtime air that's light and sweet.

You fill my days with sun so bright
That bathes the world with warmth and light.

You see my brother's tiny face,
And cover him with love and grace.

You know my pain when I get hurt
And scratch my knees on rocks and dirt.

You give me strength to keep me brave
When sometimes others misbehave.

Through oceans, mountains, rivers, plains,
All nature shows *your love* remains.

You take the time to meet me here.
Inside my heart, you're always near.

Dear God, your love is all it takes
To know I'm more than my mistakes.

When you forgive, you set me free
To be the best that I can be.

You love all creatures, big and small,
And share your glory with us all.

I see your love through young and old,
And special hands we have to hold.

I feel at peace and sense your power
In every minute, every hour.

You bless my dreams,
You bless my bed,
And the pillow where
I lay my head.

You hear my song as I drift to sleep,
And hold me in your loving keep.

God hears OUR song.

A CHILD'S PRAYER

Dear God,

I'm thankful for your love and grace
That's found in every time and place.
I'm thankful for my family, too
And pray you hold them close to you.

I'll fill my heart with lots of love
And your sweet grace from heaven above.
I'll try my hardest to be kind
To those I know and those I find.

For those who might feel sick or sad,
Please send them hope when times are bad.
I'll send my love to them as well,
For in your house, my heart does dwell.

Now and forever,
Amen

Made in United States
North Haven, CT
22 June 2023

38103034R00022